M000210256

'What he has told me has made me reassess my
relationship behaviour entirely.'
KATY REGAN, *Daily Mail*

'As if someone has just thrown a warm blanket around
my shoulders... it all makes sense.'
HANNAH BOOTH, *Guardian*

'Marshall exudes calm; his voice is gentle and measured.'
TIM DOWLING, *Guardian*

'Andrew G. Marshall offers deeply insightful, helpful,
and practical tools for dealing with most of
the challenges we face.'
JED DIAMOND, PH.D., author of
The Irritable Male Syndrome

'With advice on how to recreate
intimacy while retaining a sense of self...
His insightful advice makes it hard to disagree.'
Psychologies Magazine
(on *I Love You But I'm Not In Love With You*)

'An insightful and gracious walk through
creating positive change in your life.'
ROBERT J. ACKERMAN, PH.D., Editor,
Counselor Magazine
(on *Wake Up and Change Your Life*)

PREVIOUS TITLES BY ANDREW G. MARSHALL

I love you but I'm not in love with you:
Seven steps to saving your relationship

The single trap: The two step guide to
escaping and finding lasting love

How can I ever trust you again:
Infidelity from discovery to recovery in seven steps

Are you right for me? Seven steps to getting clarity and
commitment in your relationship

Build a life-long love affair:
Seven steps to revitalising your relationship

Heal and move on:
Seven steps to recovering from a break-up

Help your partner say yes: Seven steps to
achieving better cooperation and communication

Learn to love yourself enough: Seven steps to
improving your self-esteem and your relationships

Resolve your differences: Seven steps to
dealing with conflict in your relationship

Make love life a prairie vole: Six steps to
passionate, plentiful and monogamous sex

My wife doesn't love me any more:
Love coach guide to winning her back

I love you but you always put me last:
How to childproof your marriage

My husband doesn't love me and he's texting someone else: Love
coach guide to winning him back

Have the sex you want:
A couple's guide to getting back the spark

What is love? 50 questions about
how to find, keep and rediscover it

Wake Up and Change Your Life:
How to survive a crisis and be stronger, wiser and happier

I can't get over my partner's affair:
50 questions about recovering from extreme betrayal
and the long-term impact of infidelity

It's not a midlife crisis, it's an opportunity:
How to be forty- or fifty-something without going off the rails

CAN
WE
START
AGAIN
PLEASE?

ANDREW G. MARSHALL

CAN WE START AGAIN PLEASE?

TWENTY QUESTIONS TO FALL BACK IN LOVE

MARSHALL METHOD
PUBLISHING

Cover design by Liron Gilenberg
www.ironicitalics.com

ISBN 978-0-9955403-4-7

Find out more about the author and his books at
www.marshallmethodpublishing.com

Typeset by Elaine Sharples
typesetter@virginmedia.com

Printed in the UK by TJ International Ltd, Padstow, Cornwall

To Debby Edwards. A colleague for over twenty years

Contents

INTRODUCTION
Who is this book for?

Have you had one too many nasty rows? Does your partner feel you've let him or her down once too often? Have you drifted so far apart that saying sorry, letting time pass or doing something nice for each other will not be enough this time? If you answered yes to any of these questions, it's clear that something needs to change. If you have no real idea what that might be or no other strategy beyond trying harder, this book is for you.

I've spent over thirty years as a marital therapist helping couples in trouble and I've written eighteen books about love, infidelity and recovering from an emotional crisis. The likelihood is that I've met and worked with someone in just the same situation as you. I've taken everything I've learnt so far and stripped it back to basics: my most powerful communication strategies, three questionnaires to take stock of where you are, plus twenty questions to fall back in love or feel that first date spark again.

If you haven't read any of my books, this is a great place to start. If you've already read one of my other titles but you're looking to recruit your partner to work on your relationship, this book will help open his or her eyes, explain it is possible to fall back in love and show what needs to change. If your partner is not a big reader, busy or sceptical, the fact that this book is short – around fifteen thousand words – will be a plus point. If you're already a regular reader of my books, I want to be upfront with you. Beyond the twenty questions to fall back in love, there is nothing new here. However, this book can be used as a quick summary of my key ideas and, when you're down or doubting yourself, a way of keeping you focused and moving forward. To this end, I'm going to close the introduction with an inspirational thought – you'll find something similar at the end of each chapter. It comes from the American poet James Broughton (1913–1999): 'You must love even if it hurts. It will hurt more if you don't love.'

Andrew G. Marshall
www.andrewgmarshall.com

CHAPTER ONE

Everything you need to know about love

On the surface, everything seems fine. Every Valentine's Day you make an effort – you buy each other little presents and cards, dress up, enjoy a special meal and then go to bed with a warm glow inside. There are other memorable times of the year like a busy family Christmas or relaxing summer holidays, when you have enough time to unwind and reconnect. However, on a day-to-day basis, your relationship can be more about raising children, paying bills and doing chores than love. No wonder you sometimes ask yourself: Are we just going through the motions? Why do romantic gestures feel like such an effort when, at the beginning, we were constantly doing special little things for each other? And that nagging question; can you ever recapture that spark when you've been married decades?

Fortunately, I can reassure you that it's entirely possible. How do I know? I've spent thirty years as a marital therapist helping couples deal with the complexities of love. At the root of all the unhappiness I see, there is one problem: we know how love starts but only a hazy idea of what comes after 'happily ever after'. Understand this process and you can transform your marriage from something disappointing into something wonderful. You *can* fall back in love again.

In this short book I'm going to help you understand the issues and then show you how you can turn around your relationship, whether you've been married for three years – or thirty – and whether you want to improve what's already good, or feel you and your partner are dangerously out of touch. I've got lots of practical advice – road-tested by the three thousand clients I've helped in my career – and skills to teach that will not only protect your love from the grind of daily living but deepen your bond.

THE SIX STAGES OF LOVE

First you need to understand what happens from the tentative first 'I love you' through to spending a lifetime together. Relationships go through six specific stages and understanding them is key because for love to last it needs something different at each one. And whether you've been together since you were teenagers, or met later in life, your relationship will go through the same stages (though second-time around the middle stages are shorter).

1. *Blending* (From six to eighteen months)

This is a magical time when it feels like you're walking on air, can't think of anything but your beloved and even his or her failings are endearing. Psychologists call this 'limerence' – and it's not just in your head. Research has shown this emotional high is caused by chemical changes in the body. By scanning the brains of those in the first flush of love, neuroscientists have found that bonding hormones like oxytocin and dopamine are at their height during this stage. To give you an idea of the power, researchers at Bar-Ilan University found oxytocin levels were double for new couples compared with singles. However, the seeds of later problems can be sown during Blending because any differences between the two of you are overlooked as you fuse into one couple. And if there's a row it feels like the end of the world because unlike settled couples, you've no experience of falling out, disagreeing and making up together.

> **Targeted Tip:** For those starting a new relationship later in life you're probably feeling like a teenager again, which is exciting, but it's likely you also feel vulnerable. To give you confidence to overcome any disputes, it helps to think back to the first year of a past relationship and think about what you argued about and how you solved those problems.
>
> Even if you have been married for decades, you can still get a boost of limerence – although it lasts for a much shorter time – when you kiss and forgive after a serious

argument. So although, like new couples, you are worried about being honest (because of the potential fallout) if you do raise hot button topics, there is a double benefit. Nothing can be solved if you don't talk about it and making up again brings back the sweetness of stage one love.

2. *Nesting* (Eighteen months to three years)

Limerence is beginning to wear off but there's still enough left for you to want to hitch your destiny to a comparative stranger. Although, in my experience, it has declined by about 25%, that feels more comfortable after the almost manic edge of love in stage one. Sexual desire moves from something constant onto a more settled level. You're aware of life beyond the bedroom and creating a home together becomes the new way to express your love. In fact, long-term tracking by the University of Texas suggests eighteen months to three years is the optimum courtship period for a happy marriage. Meanwhile social biologists believe that our brains are wired for a three-year peak to help us find a mate and care for the babies when they are small and helpless.

> **Targeted Tip:** If your boyfriend or girlfriend is unsure about a deeper commitment and says 'We're happy as we are', it is important to listen to his or her fears. Rather than trying to reassure or reason, ask questions: 'What makes you feel like that?' Prompt your beloved to open up by

nodding your head or saying: 'Tell me more'. After a while, he or she will start to soothe his or her own fears and become less entrenched. Finally, tell your beloved, 'Living together is important to my happiness' and leave it to settle for a month or two.

If you've been married for years, it is still helpful to look back because the seeds for discontentment today could have been planted at this stage. When you first moved in together, you probably copied what your mother and father did around the house – without thinking about it. Take a fresh look at who does what and whether the gender stereotypes work for you and your partner today. He or she might be happy doing something you hate.

3. *Self-affirming* (Third or fourth year)

A UK poll of 3,000 engaged or married couples found the average length between the first meeting and accepting a proposal is two years and eleven months. So most couples get married during this stage. It's likely that by now you're feeling confident enough about the relationship to enjoy separate activities again. After all, it does not take two people to go to the D.I.Y. store and choose a hammer! Not only is it natural for your individual traits, habits and characteristics to re-emerge but the long-term health of your relationship demands it. If you don't express your personal needs, you risk resenting your partner or feeling controlled. However, it's really hard to balance your needs and the relationship's needs. Sometimes couples think the inevitable rows mean their love is doomed but you've begun to knock each other's rough edges off and have a relationship based on the reality of who you are (rather than trying to change each other into your image of the perfect partner).

> **Targeted Tip:** However long you've been together, I can't underline strongly enough the importance of arguing effectively. It is the most important skill I teach my clients. Without it, you are likely to fall into one of the four negative behaviours that researchers at the University of Washington found bring a 90% likelihood of divorce. These are defensiveness, stonewalling, emotional withdrawal and contempt (from feeling superior to your partner). So instead of agreeing to what your partner wants (being passive) or demanding what you want (domineering), I stress assertiveness where both of your needs are equally important. I sum it up by using this mantra: 'I can ask, you can say no and we can negotiate' (by which I mean compromise or trade something you want for something your partner wants). If you find it hard not to give in and please your partner, take a couple of deep breaths and say 'maybe' rather than 'no' and keep talking.

4. *Collaborating* (Fifth to fourteenth year)

You use the sense of security and self-esteem boost from the relationship to take on a big project. It could be a career change, going back to college or simply new interests. Alternatively, the project can be a joint one – like starting a family. When it comes to couples who meet later in life, from the ones I've met it's very common to launch a business or renovate a cottage in the countryside together, or simply do a lot of travelling. I call this Collaborating because of the support you offer each other and because the excitement and freshness generated is brought back into the relationship and shared.

> **Targeted Tip:** While it's often an exciting time this is also the hardest stage for couples as you can get wrapped up in an outside project and neglect your partner. It's no coincidence that the average length of a failed marriage in the UK is 11.3 years. It sounds obvious, but so many people forget to include their partner. So make a special effort to invite your other half to special events in your world and show an interest in or help with his or her projects. It's good advice no matter how long you've been together. I've counselled wives who have been involved in the P.T.A. at their children's schools and encouraged their men to pitch in too – for example, by offering to run the barbecue at the fête. I've also had women who have decided to ride pillion on their husbands' motorcycles on special trips – like along Route 66 in the USA.

5. *Adapting* (Fifteen to twenty-five years)
This is a stage of two extremes. It's likely you're adapting to

challenges thrown at you – like children leaving home or ageing parents – rather than coping with changes in the relationship. This can leave you feeling self-absorbed and with little space for your partner or for fun. But it can also be a time of sexual awakening as with maturity – many women find the menopause liberates them as the risk of pregnancy is gone. Many men stop trying to prove themselves and become more responsive to their wives' desires – rather than what they think she wants. Both men and women, by this stage of life, care less what other people will think and can be more honest about their needs in the bedroom.

Targeted Tip: It is important to break old habits and open yourself up for new experiences. Start by doing something relatively easy – like swapping places round the kitchen table. How does it feel to sit in your partner's seat? You could also have different chairs to watch TV. When I quiz my couples, I'm surprised by how few are on the sofa together. If you're not doing it, lie in each other's arms instead of being marooned in separate spaces. When you go to the cinema together, chose a film at random. Make love in a room in your home where you've never done it before. Go to bed an hour earlier. Choose an activity you haven't done for ages – like going for a swim together. At the end of a month of doing things differently, have a thirty-minute meeting to discuss what happened, decide what activities to keep and plan more adventures.

6. *Renewing* (Twenty-five years plus)

Older couples can be the most romantic. It's like an echo of Blending but while the first stage is based on the promise of a lifetime together, renewing draws on the reality and the strength that comes from overcoming obstacles. You also feel a shared sense of achievement in raising a family together and pride in your grandchildren. However, it is easy to be overwhelmed by other people's demands – particularly for childcare or from grown-up children who have boomeranged back home. Therefore it is important to be able to say no and keep back enough energy for doing something exciting together.

> **Targeted Tip:** Draw on the past memories by going back to places that were romantically significant, get out your wedding photos and watch the holiday videos or go dancing together.

QUIZ
How Strong is Your Love?

Research shows if you compare your marriage to other
people's, you'll judge your own to be better. However,
focusing selectively on what is bad in friends' marriages and
what is good in your own produces a superiority bias where
you're fine but everyone else is messed up. Over three decades
as a marital therapist, I've identified key questions that get
to the heart of a relationship and whether it's functioning
well or hanging by a thread. I've incorporated these into a
test so you can find out what's really going on in yours:

1 When you see each other again after a day at work (or
   some other short separation) how do you feel?
   a) Anxious about how things will go between us.
   b) Generally stressed because there's supper to make,
       kids' homework to supervise, etc.
   c) Not much until I've had enough time to unwind.
   d) A small surge of happiness.

2 How happy are you both with the amount of sex that
   you're having?
   a) It's not something I've ever really thought about.
   b) One of us feels pressured for sex and the other that
       he or she is frequently turned down.

c)   More would be nice but things are generally OK when we get round to it.

d)   Sex is good and we're both equally committed to making it a priority.

3   When your partner is distant, how do you react?
   a)   Let him or her get on with it.
   b)   I worry that I've done something wrong.
   c)   I'm concerned but if I say anything I'll probably be fobbed off.
   d)   I ask what's the matter.

4   How much does your partner believe in you and support your projects?
   a)   I sometimes feel really alone.
   b)   He or she is supportive – until I ask for something (like help with childcare or time away).
   c)   My partner can sometimes be dismissive or teases me about them.
   d)   Really supportive, I can talk over any concerns.

5   How do you handle disagreements?
   a)   One of us gets really upset and cries, shouts or goes off in a huff.
   b)   We go round in circles until one of us brokers peace but often things aren't properly sorted.
   c)   We don't really have any disagreements.

   d) We can talk through our differences, listen to each
      other and find a solution together.

6 What happens when there is an important decision to
  be made – like choosing a school for the children or
  buying something expensive?
   a) There's lots of arguments and resentment.
   b) The person who's on the spot, or knows most about
      the topic, makes the call.
   c) One of us does the necessary research but consults
      the other before making a decision.
   d) We're a team and everything is done jointly.

7 How has your relationship been over the past twelve
  months?
   a) Difficult. My partner or I have been prickly,
      dismissive or out more than usual.
   b) Incredibly busy, we've barely had time to talk
      beyond functional conservations about running the
      house or what time to pick up the kids.
   c) The usual ups and downs.
   d) We've been really close.

Mostly a) In need of intense care
It's likely that you knew your marriage was in a dark place
before doing this test, but it's also likely that you have no idea
how to make things better. While you would probably benefit

from some professional help, there are strategies you can try that will help improve the situation. Start by thinking of how you've raised issues that are bothering you with your partner. I expect that you've ended up listing or describing the problems – and that this has made your partner defensive and angry. Next time, instead of concentrating on everything that's wrong, focus on solutions and achieving them together. For example: How are we going to resolve our relationship problems? What changes do we need to make? If you find yourselves getting upset, it probably means you've stopped asking open questions. Take a few deep breaths and if you're feeling calmer ask: Why is this so difficult? Alternatively, take a break and come back to the discussion later. Don't underestimate the power of making small changes in the way you communicate. There is still hope for turning round your relationship.

Mostly b) Looking peaky

You love each other – and that's great. However, you're taking it for granted that bedrock of love will support you through the issues such as being wrapped up in your job or the children, and the general stresses in life. However love needs skills as well as connection. Perhaps the most important one is listening. Each time you feel tempted to interrupt, bite the inside of your cheek and nod your head. When your partner has finished, summarise what he or she said, so you can be sure you heard what he or she meant rather than what you thought was meant. They are often two different things.

Mostly c) Fine

With medical tests there's 'fine fine,' and 'fine, but we need to key an eye on things' and you fall into this category. You have good communication skills – which are vital for relationship health – but they might need brushing up. The research from the University of Washington about divorce predictors also found it takes five nice things (smiling, compliments, flirty texts, saying thank you, hugs) to combat a single nasty one (being short, sarcastic comments, not looking up from your smartphone) but I've found among my clients that ratio of ten to one helps love to thrive. How easy is this to do? Harder than you think? How could you up your score?

Mostly d) Strong and healthy

Life is hard but you have each other's backs. You know how to communicate effectively and sort problems out before they become serious. Rather than being complacent, take a deeper look at your relationship. Are there what I call 'buried bodies' – subjects that both of you know are an issue but you don't raise them for fear of what might happen? For example, one of you does not like the other's mother. If you talk about them, they will be less scary and less potentially harmful.

EXERCISES

How to flirt with your partner

When you've been together years, flirting – making your partner aware that they're attractive to you – gets overlooked in the day-to-day grind of life. Think about the last time you had a five-minute cuddle in the middle of the day or walked hand in hand down the street – the chances are it's longer than you think. The secret is to start with something small, at the non-sexual end of the spectrum, and build slowly. Check your partner's reaction and then move onto something more explicit.

Build passion while apart. Leave a message where only your partner will find it or send a saucy text message. It doesn't even have to be sexual if you're uncomfortable with that, just fun and playful or even 'Guess what I'm cooking you for tea?'

Casual touching. When couples have been together a long time they tend to become less tactile. Rub your leg against his or hers in a restaurant, gently touch your partner's face or stroke his or her hair.

Teasing each other. Play peekaboo: (i.e. peer from behind the menu and then hide your eyes). Tickling each other might sound childish, but it makes you laugh and builds a physical connection.

Playful kisses. Again, passionate kisses nearly always become pecks on the cheek in long-term relationships. When was the last time you properly smooched your other half? Give an extra long-kiss when your partner comes home, and try kissing with your eyes open. Or try kissing in a way you don't normally do – e.g. fluttery kisses on the neck.

How to be more romantic

Romance is showing your partner that you care, and it doesn't have to be sexual, but its power is increased by novelty so you need to keep looking for fresh ways to express your love.

Increase sensuality. Read a poem out loud. Build a campfire and stare at the flames. Offer to massage his or her shoulders after a difficult day at work.

Add an extra dimension to the ordinary. Take your partner out for breakfast, or turn up at work and take him or her for lunch, dress up even though you're staying in.

The power of three. Take something you already do but add extra dimensions. For example, collect your partner from the station but have a bottle of champagne and an ice bucket in the back of the car and stop somewhere scenic on the way home.

Get a little help. Watching a scary movie together (the tension will make you hold onto each other) or slow dance to your partner's favourite crooner.

Small presents. The unexpected present is more powerful than the expected one, and it doesn't have to be big. It just has to show that you care enough to notice their likes and dislikes. Leave a chocolate on the pillow or buy your other half their favourite wine, or biscuits, when you're next in the supermarket.

CLOSING THOUGHT

'Thinking too well of people often allows them to behave better than they otherwise would.' Anti-apartheid leader and president of South Africa, Nelson Mandela (1918– 2013).

The temptation is to criticise your partner – which can easily encourage him or her to live down to his or her reputation for being lazy, selfish or whatever. What would happen if you praised him or her – or in the words of Mandela 'think too well' – would it encourage your partner to live up to this better image?

CHAPTER TWO

Why we fall out of love

We think it's the big issues that drive a wedge between couples – like financial problems, infidelity or disagreements about how many children to have. However, I've spent three decades helping couples in crisis and while we might retrospectively put relationship breakdowns down to major events, what I see over and over again is that it's the accumulation of little things that destroys love. Whether it's repeatedly working late because you think it's more important to be financially secure than spending evenings with your partner or something as mundane as shouting requests to each other from different rooms. And who hasn't done that?

In this chapter, I'm going address the habits that seem harmless but have the power to undo even the strongest bonds and why you shouldn't panic if your other half tells you they don't love you any more.

FIVE BAD HABITS THAT ARE
SABOTAGING YOUR LOVE

Your relationship will survive one of these bad habits without too many ill effects, maybe even two, but once you reach three you're building up long-term problems.

1. Having to be right all the time

It's really easy to spot when your partner is falling into this trap. For example, you can't even mention a little problem – like leaving the kitchen in a mess after cooking – because he or she will fly off the handle and claim: 'I was just about to clear it up'. However, you are just as likely to be guilty yourself. When your partner pulls you up on something, how often do you say 'yes, but' or have a ready-made excuse?

This goes right back to childhood and our reaction when our parents got angry or told us off. They didn't mean to give the message 'If you're naughty, I won't love you' but to immature brains that's the conclusion we jumped to. So even though, as adults, we intellectually know that our partner will still love us even if we make a mistake, we tend to become overcome by shame and cover up these uncomfortable feelings by claiming to be right.

> **Break the habit:** Couples in my practice will sometimes turn round their whole relationship with one simple change: apologising when they've slipped up. Don't lessen

the power by explaining why – because this sounds like an excuse for bad behaviour, just say 'I'm sorry that I left the kitchen in a mess' and leave it at that. (If it still feels important twenty-four hours later, you can give your partner all the background. However, in my experience, you won't remember why you were bent out of shape.)

2. Zoning out

It could be staying glued to the TV or your phone while your partner is trying to tell you something, or thinking about work when she's going through childcare arrangements because you're not really interested (or think 'That's her job'). You tell yourself 'It will only take a minute to finish this email' or 'My programme will be over in ten minutes' and 'We have the whole evening together' but by not paying attention you give a clear message: 'I'm not that interested' or 'Other people and things are more important than you'. This is a far cry from when you fell in love and every waking moment seemed to revolve around each other.

Break the habit: It sounds easy but actually this tip is really hard to follow through: always be in the same room when you speak to each other. You'll find you want to shout up the stairs – which sounds like a command rather than a request. Or you'll want to say something from the door rather than going into the room where your partner is working. But by entering and waiting until your partner notices and looks up, you will feel truly heard.

3. Tiptoeing round your partner

You are so determined to keep the peace that if your husband or wife gets huffy when, for example, you want to go out with your friends, rather than challenging him or her – and getting everything out in the open – you turn down invitations. This doesn't just apply to large issues either, but seemingly petty domestic rules. Take how the towels are folded in the bathroom. Your partner may insist on them being done in a particular way, and while you either don't really care or are irritated by his or her obsessive standards – you say nothing and go along with them. Nobody likes arguments but disagreeing with your partner makes you feel particularly uncomfortable. However, you do have the right to give your opinion.

This passive behaviour is usually learned from the way your parents interacted. Either you had a front row seat while your parents ripped each other apart (which made you determined not to fall into the same trap) or they never argued (and you don't know how to disagree, argue and make up). So the only way to keep things running smoothly is to turn off any annoyance. The problem is that once you start shutting feelings down then eventually you shut down the positive ones, like love, too.

> **Break the habit:** Start with something small – like your partner slurping his tea – which you'd normally let go or tell yourself 'it's no big deal' even though it irritates the hell

out of you. Experiment and tell your partner – when it's happening and something can be done about it – and see what happens.

So how do you tell them? If you go round the houses and build up to it gradually, your partner will think something terrible is about to be said. Don't make a joke of it either, as this lessens the impact and your complaint might not be taken seriously. Just say: would you mind drinking your tea more quietly? My guess is that he or she will not be too upset – especially if it is something small – but you will feel really great. Many of my clients say it's like a weight lifted off their shoulders because they hadn't realised how angry small things made them. They also start feeling empowered and confident about tackling bigger issues.

4. Putting the children first

Children need a lot – especially when they're babies – but they grow up and somehow everything in the house still seems to revolve around them. It's not in doubt that you both want what's best for your offspring. However, you got married because you had fun together, not to spend weeks on end when the only meaningful conversation is about when to pick up your son or daughter. Lots of people think this is a trap that only women fall into and it's men who feel resentful. However, I have couselled just as many women who feel shut out sometimes by their husbands or always the disciplinarian as Dad raises his eyebrows to his kids when Mum tells them to stop playing football with him and do their homework. There might be lots of family time but have you been so busy being Mum and Dad that you've forgotten to be lovers too?

> **Break the habit:** Our culture is so child centred – and we're so terrified of making a mistake – that when I suggested the following tip on a daytime TV programme I had both hosts and the other guest screaming at me! So what is it? Greet your partner first when you come home and don't let the kids interrupt when you're talking to each other. If I've made you angry too, it probably means that I've hit a nerve, but many couples tell me these simple rules have helped them refocus on each other. Don't forget your children are just passing through while marriage is forever.

5. Keeping score

If you think you're in a fairly happy marriage you're unlikely to own up to this one, but in my experience *everybody* has a secret score card in their head. For men, it sounds something like this: 'I earn the majority of the money that pays for everything, I do way more housework than my father and I'm a really involved dad, but what thanks do I get?' For women it goes: 'I earn too, I run the house, know the children's teachers' names and make their costumes for Victorian Day at school. I even buy birthday presents for his mother and what does he do in return?' We understand our position so well and know all our female or male friends would back us up, we're certain we're right – even though that automatically puts our partner in the wrong.

> **Break the habit:** Look at the division of tasks with fresh eyes. I ask my clients to make a list of everything they do and then swap over – it can make very sobering reading as both sides underestimate what the other does. Discuss what in particular makes you feel overloaded and listen to your partner's problem areas. If you can agree to take one thing off your partner's list and give them one of yours, you will clear the air and start to be a team again.

FIVE GOOD HABITS TO PROTECT YOUR LOVE

It's tempting to rely on love as the magic potion to protect your relationship from harm – after all the pop songs constantly tell us 'all you need is love' and 'love will build a bridge' or variations on that theme. However, love is a living thing that needs to be fed or it will wither and die. Here's how to keep it nourished.

1. Check in regularly with each other

Ideally this should be on a daily basis, perhaps set aside five minutes at the beginning of the evening or decide to eat together (at a table, with TV and smartphones switched off). Chat about what you've been up to and flag up anything that is causing stress – otherwise your partner might think it's all about them, when actually you're preoccupied with work. I recommend having a relationship 'board meeting' at least once every six months to discuss your dreams and aspirations. You could even make an evening of it and go somewhere nice together.

2. Be curious

When you first started dating, you'd want to know everything about each other. If he or she loved Canadian ice hockey, or something equally obscure, you'd probably even choose a team to support. Now you assume you know everything about each other. If you find something boring – like your partner's job or hobby – it's probably because you don't know enough. Ask for a guided tour of your partner's work, ask lots of questions about how things are done and get introduced to all the work colleagues. Or go along to his rallycross event, or sit in on her choir rehearsal and go for a drink with her friends afterwards.

3. Go the extra mile

It's human nature to take what we have for granted, so although the everyday stuff is important – like washing, cleaning, gardening, maintaining the car, etc. – it blends into the background. What we notice is something beyond the call of duty. You'd be amazed how many marriages have been turned round by men taking a day off work to cover a childcare emergency. Don't be fobbed off by your partner saying 'I can manage' because this 'failure' to help – for example, letting your partner take a taxi home after a minor operation instead of collecting her yourself, as one client of mine did – will be remembered long into the future.

4. Share an interest
My mantra is the couple who plays together stays together. It could be joining something that your partner enjoys (like cycling) and developing this into a joint challenge (cycling through the French Alps) or starting something together from scratch (like scuba diving or learning a foreign language). Don't worry if this is going to stretch you because research shows that overcoming obstacles and adversity is more bonding than just sharing nice things together (like a luxury spa break).

5. Make sex a priority
I am often shocked to discover both halves of a couple have been lying on their separate side of the bed wishing the other would make the first move. Sex is important because it is not only bonding but repairs the damage caused by arguments and creates a sense of me and you against the world. Don't wait for your partner to initiate love-making and in the next chapter I will explain how to recapture that spark and reconnect sexually.

'I DON'T LOVE YOU ANY MORE' DOESN'T HAVE TO MEAN THE END

You knew things weren't great but you'd no idea it had reached this stage. Your partner has either said 'I love you but I'm not in love with you' or come right out with it and declared the marriage over. You'll probably be in shock and think your world is crumbling around you. However, trust me, it's not as bad as you fear. I find more marriages end at this point, not because one partner is determined to leave, but in their panic their spouse pushes them out of the door.

You will have made mistakes about the way you handled the news – I've yet to meet someone in your situation who hasn't. What counts is that you identify what isn't working so you can stop and try something different.

Don't...

> ***Talk about love.*** It's wonderful that you still love your partner, because it will provide the determination to turn round your marriage, but repeatedly telling him or her is just a reminder that he or she doesn't love you. Don't bring up love again until your partner wants to talk about it.
>
> ***Beg for a second chance.*** In your partner's eyes, begging makes you look pathetic and strengthens his or her belief that you're not the one for them.
>
> ***Go for a quick fix.*** You're on the internet booking a

romantic trip on the Orient Express, but this just shows you're not listening. It makes your partner think you've not taken the enormity of his or her decision seriously.

Use the children. It's not just you who's going to be heartbroken but the kids too. You've also read somewhere that children from divorced homes do worse in school – and make sure your husband or wife knows this. But this tactic will either push your partner further away (because he or she has probably thought of nothing but the effect on the kids and you're suggesting he or she hasn't) or you'll be fobbed off with 'they'll get over it' (which makes you mad and causes another row).

Label your partner as the problem. There might be some truth in this diagnosis but telling your partner where he or she is going wrong is not going to rekindle love, just make him or her defensive. It also makes you feel helpless because you can't change someone else. However, if you think of this as a problem with your marriage – a joint problem – you can start fixing your half.

Do...

It might take two people to fix a marriage but you can start the ball rolling. That way your partner is encouraged to want to mend it too. Here's how...

> *Acknowledge.* You can never say phrases like these enough – 'I can see you're unhappy', 'I know you're angry' or 'I didn't listen in the past'. Demonstrate how much you want to understand with follow-up questions: 'How did that feel?' Meanwhile, prompts like 'Tell me more' show you can listen – even to difficult and painful subjects. Over time, it will raise a small flicker of hope in your partner's heart: change might be possible.
>
> *Imagine every word he or she says is true:* For a second, imagine that everything your partner says is right – because in his or her head they will be. How does the situation look now? What would you change about your behaviour?
>
> *Make a concrete plan.* Take everything you've learnt from your discussions since your partner announced the bombshell and write down what you personally need to do differently – as this will underline your commitment. Make certain the changes are SMART: Specific, measurable, achievable, realistic and timed (i.e. there's a date for completion). You might like to tell your partner your resolution – it's up to you – but be prepared for him or her to be sceptical.

Be kind to yourself. It will take time to turn things round and it will be harder if you're not eating or sleeping properly. In addition, it's easy to take your partner's criticism too much to heart and think it's ALL your fault. In thirty years of helping people in your situation, I've yet to meet a couple where it is not six of one and half a dozen of the other and I doubt you're the exception.

Get the right help. An outside eye will help you stay balanced and provide support when you're down. However, choose carefully. Don't confide in your children and drag them into the dispute and your mother might not be the most neutral observer. Find a friend who's been through something similar – but either stayed with, or is on good terms with, his or her partner – or consult a professional.

EXERCISE

Are you feeding or depleting your marriage?

Think back to when your marriage was fine – perhaps three to five years ago. What did you do then that fed your marriage? Think about your marriage today. What activities exhaust or stress you out and deplete you and your marriage?

Write it down. Seeing everything on a piece of paper provides a clearer perspective. Put what fed (or still feeds) you down on one side and what depletes you on the other.

What could you do less? Is there something on the depletes side that you could stop or make less of a priority – like working in the evening?

What could you do more? Now you've remembered how good things used to be, how could you bring back the activities that you've dropped – like phoning up old friends and arranging to meet up? If your partner doesn't want to do stuff with you at the moment, choose something to feed yourself and keep you strong. If your partner is up for a 'no pressure' date or simply having fun together, this could be a shared activity.

CLOSING THOUGHT

'Be patient toward all that is unsolved in your heart and to try to love the questions themselves... Live the questions now. Perhaps you will then gradually, without noticing it, live along some distant day into the answer.' Bohemian-Austrian poet Rainer Maria Rilke (1875–1926)

You might think you need to have all the answers – right now, today or at the latest by the weekend. But if you press yourself (or your partner), fear gets in the way and the answer becomes no. But if you can learn to be OK with uncertainty and even, as Rilke suggests, love the questions, you will live into the answer. How do I know? Because I've worked with lots of people who have learnt to ask themselves: how did we get to this point, what can we do differently and what changes could I make (rather than waiting for my partner to make the first move)? And, guess what, they all lived into the answer.

CHAPTER THREE

How to get the spark back in your sex life

Loaded looks, lingering kisses – and then you and your partner fall into each other's arms and the cares of the day melt away. It sounds great, doesn't it? However, from what I've learned about long-term relationships, I wouldn't be surprised if that passionate, connected love-making rarely happens. If it does it's most likely when you're on holiday or on a weekend away – when you're both relaxed and have time for each other. All too often, sex is the last thing on your mind after a long and busy day and instead of bonding you together, it becomes another thing on a never-ending to-do list, a source of arguments or off-limits altogether.

However, once the myths about sex (like it's all athleticism between the sheets) have been challenged and all your fears (can I satisfy my partner, does he or she still fancy me?) have been addressed, sex can become not just one of the greatest pleasures but the glue that binds you together and stops you from becoming 'just friends'.

So in this chapter, based on the practical advice that's been road-tested by my clients, I'm going to explain how you *can* put the passion back into even the most lacklustre love life and rebuild the intimacy between the two of you.

KNOW THE RULES FOR TALKING ABOUT SEX

The better you know someone, surely the easier it is to talk about sex? But, surprising as it may sound, the opposite is likely to be true with your partner. Many of the couples that I counsel are left guessing what each other likes or dislikes depending on a conversation they had fifteen years ago or more, when they first met. Unfortunately, when we're together with someone for a long time, we develop a shorthand for communicating – sometimes as if we can read each other's minds – but while it might make day-to-day domestic life easier, this can be a negative when it comes to intimacy. Over the years people's needs and desires change, but your partner won't know if you don't share them. So here's how to update your sex life for the people you are today.

Don't talk about sex in the bedroom. Although your bedroom is a private space, it is too loaded for such an intimate topic. If the conversation happens after sex, your partner will take it as a bad review and if you're getting into bed, it could be seen as an invitation to make love. I recommend a long car journey alone together (less eye contact can make talking easier) or over dinner (eating can cover potentially embarrassing silences or provide thinking time).

Break the ice. Try this fun game that is used to help train sex therapists. Take a piece of paper and write down as many words you can come up with for the male and female genitals (from the coy terms you used as kids, through the dirty ones to the over-the-top ones from romantic novels) and the same for having sex. It will get you laughing and that brings down the barriers and builds creativity.

Concentrate on the positive. We all have insecurities, so even the most innocuous statements can be heard as criticism. So 'I need to talk about sex' becomes 'You're rubbish in bed' or 'We need to spice things up' is 'I'm thinking of having an affair'. So start with an unambiguously positive statement: 'I really enjoy our love-making' or remember a particularly good occasion: 'Do you remember that four-poster bed in Paris?' and explain what you liked. Follow up with a question that invites your partner to think creatively: How can we build on that? If you have any complaints, turn it round and put it as a positive. Instead of 'You're rushing me and I can't relax' turn it round with 'I love it when you're slow and take your time'.

Avoid words that raise the stakes. As soon as you say 'never' or 'always', your partner will get defensive or find the one exception. Own your statements: 'I feel' instead of 'You make me feel'.

Be as specific as possible. When my clients first talk about sex, they talk about it in such general terms that sometimes I have no idea what they mean. So be as precise as possible. Instead of saying 'I'd like longer cuddles' try saying 'I'd like to cuddle for ten minutes' or your partner could think you mean hours of foreplay. If your partner says something upsetting, ask him or her to explain, or ask a question. You might have jumped to the wrong conclusion.

Show rather than tell. A touch is worth a thousand words, so take your partner's hand and put it where you'd like to be caressed, or use it to show when you prefer firmer or lighter pressure. When it feels good, let out a moan or a sigh so you're giving positive reinforcement.

THREE BARRIERS TO DESIRE

Lots of couples have a guilty secret that they wouldn't even tell their best friend, and certainly won't discuss together.

This secret is that once a couple has the right number of children for their family, sex happens so sporadically it's probably less than ten times a year – what sex therapists call a low-sex relationship. This applies to about one in five marriages. Most couples blames circumstances – stress, tiredness, etc. – but these are excuses; often it's down to their attitudes and behaviour.

1. Unrealistic expectations

We have all sorts of expectations about how sex should be. In most cases, these are so deeply ingrained that most of my clients don't know they hold them. So I often get them to complete this sentence: 'Sex should...' The most common answer is 'Sex should happen naturally' but when you have a family nothing happens spontaneously – not at least without a lot of groundwork first! Other couples worry that 'Sex should always be special' so hold back until everything is perfect, except that the perfect time never comes. And what they don't realise is that a quickie can be just as much fun. Perhaps the most damaging expectation is that 'A couple doesn't need to have sex to have a good marriage' – as this allows a low-sex relationship to drift into a no-sex one. Of course, no one should be pressured into having sex they don't want but equally no one should have to do without the sex they *do* want.

Turn it round: To keep a healthy and vibrant love life forget spontaneity, you need to plan ahead and make a sex date. Of course, if one of you is under the weather, you can reorganise but always agree a new date and still use the time to do something nice together – like sharing a long, hot bath.

2. Pestering

Alan Riley is professor of sexual health at the University of Lancashire and he tracked levels of desire in a large sample and plotted them on a graph from highest to lowest. The majority of us lie in the middle but Riley found that, in general, women tend to fall somewhere on the lower end and men, in general, on the higher end. Therefore a typical woman in a relationship with a typical man will want sex less often than he does. Unfortunately, in a bid to get the sex he wants this makes him likely to not only drop repeated hints, but make sarcastic comments or crude remarks – which is a huge turn-off for his partner or leads to duty sex (which doesn't really satisfy him and damages her libido). Worse still, his wife is also more likely to repel all touch – whether sexual or not – because she's worried that it might lead to intercourse.

Turn it round: You can get round the 'all or nothing' trap by agreeing a cuddle can be just a cuddle – not an invitation to sex. Agree places where loving touch –

stroking and massages – are just that (for example, on the sofa). In this way, you can both relax and enjoy the moment without worrying if you're going to get lucky or feel pestered.

3. Resentment

Many desire problems have their origins outside the bedroom. If you're the principal breadwinner, you can feel that your hard work isn't properly appreciated. When it comes to running the house and organising childcare, it's easy for the partner doing the lion's share to feel unsupported. However, instead of rocking the boat, most people swallow their dissatisfaction or let it seep out with barbed comments – either way it leads to the biggest turn-off of all: resentment.

Turn it round: If you can talk about issues, this not only resolves them but stops another layer of resentment being added. Try explaining your position using the formula: *I feel...* (so your partner doesn't imagine something worse) *when you...* (so reassures your partner it doesn't happen all the time) *because...* (so he or she doesn't assume the wrong reason). For example, I feel annoyed when you check your phone in front of me because it makes me think you'd rather be somewhere else.

QUIZ
Test Your Sexual Style

Great sex is not just about connecting physically but emotionally too. However, there are three different meanings that we place on love-making and understanding yours and your partner's makes all the difference between a functional and a rewarding experience. There is no right or wrong choice, and no style is better than the other, it's down to personal preference.

1   My ideal love-making is:
    a) An expression of love for my partner.
    b) A trip into a world of sensory stimulation and
        tingling nerve endings.
    c) A drama that begins with attraction, develops a plot
        filled with intrigue and mystery and ends with a
        tumultuous release.

2   I'm most likely to be in the mood for passionate sex
    when:
    a) I'm feeling really loving towards my partner.
    b) I'm physically relaxed and mentally receptive.
    c) I'm feeling playful and adventurous.

3   When it comes to the perfect place for making love,
    I would choose:

a) Somewhere that has special meaning for me and my partner.
b) Somewhere that ensures total privacy.
c) A semi-public place to make secret love.

4 The type of pillow talk that I prefer is:
   a) Compliments, and, best of all, 'I love you'.
   b) Moans and sighs are great but talking distracts from the moment.
   c) Urging, begging, or 'talking dirty'.

5 If I was going to play music during sex, I would choose something:
   a) Lyrical, romantic, and poetic to match my partner's loving mood.
   b) Soft and low that facilitates the mood without setting a pace to be followed.
   c) Dramatic and exciting rhythms that frame and feed my fantasies.

6 When it comes to fantasies, I'm most likely to enjoy:
   a) The idea that my partner is pledging his or her love and devotion through sex.
   b) Using my imagination to sink further into the sensual experience.
   c) The novelty of imagining different activities, settings, and positions.

7 Pick the emotion you most associate with sex:
   a) Love.
   b) Enjoyment.
   c) Excitement.

Mostly a) Partner focused

Sex is all about how you feel about each other. You like to stare into your partner's eyes during love-making and enjoy intimate conversations before, during and after sex. You like to be completely present and if your partner drifts off into a private world (see Trance) or suggests something different (see Creative), you can take it as personal insult. Try instead to see it as a matter of taste and discuss how you could indulge your partner sometimes and still be true to yourself.

Mostly b) Trance

You like to sink into the moment and lose yourself in the sensations of making love. You enjoy slow and repetitive movements to help you relax and let yourself go. For you, opening your eyes (see Partner focused) or games (see Creative) is a distraction. Explain your preferences to your partner and look for a middle way where you can be generous and give something in his or her style at the beginning of love-making but in the later stages you're allowed to float into your private world of bliss.

Mostly c) Creative

Sex is an adventure and you enjoy role play, games and dressing up. Variety is important to you and therefore you're happy to go along with your partner's style but don't forget to ask for what you need too.

Mixture

You enjoy all the different styles of love-making but look at the descriptions and see if there's something you'd like to explore further.

REINVIGORATE YOUR LOVE LIFE – GO ON A SEX DIET

This is going to come as a shock: sometimes the best way to put the spark back is to stop having sex for a month. My clients are often astonished: 'We're hardly having sex and you're asking us to stop'. I know it sounds counter-intuitive but there are three main reasons to stop having intercourse or other sexual contact:

1 It reduces tension between you and your partner.
2 It helps you get in touch with the full range of sensual pleasures.
3 The diet involves talking about sex and that's good for your overall communication.

Week One: Cuddles

Raising a family, earning a living, and running a household are so tiring that we can demote love-making to the bottom of our list of priorities. Unfortunately, this can make you or your partner feel unwanted or unimportant. Cuddling and sensual touch can begin to repair this damage, as one is never too tired to be held.

So for the first week stick to cuddles and non-sexual touching. Discuss whether you want to be naked or keep your underwear on. Take it in turns to stroke and massage your partner's body. I ask for at least ten minutes each for touching or being touched (but longer is fine). Discover what kind of touching gets the best response. Does firmer pressure or a light touch work better for you or your other half? Where do you particularly enjoy being stroked?

Stop if you feel the desire to take things further. While these are good signs, the idea is to discover the pleasure of being touched all over your body and if you become sexual you could overwhelm the subtler but still important sensations. End with a cuddle and discuss the experience and your reactions (especially the unexpected ones).

Week Two: Sensual Kissing

Beyond a peck on the lips, many couples abandon sensual kissing once they're in a settled relationship, focusing instead on the sexual act. So why does it happen? Partly, we think snogging is for teenagers and now we're grown up and serious – and can go all the way – we overlook the fun of the preliminary stages. However, on your sex diet you can really enjoy kissing for kissing's sake and discover how important it is for building desire.

For the second week continue with the touching you did in week one, but find new places to kiss your partner. What about the neck or the elbow? Take it in turns to experiment with different kinds of kisses – light, intense, nibbly, etc. Like before, finish with a cuddle and, again, give each other feedback.

Week Three: Sensual Touching
Elicit different sensations by stroking each other with fabrics (for example, a piece of velvet, silk, or faux fur) and give each other plenty of feedback about what feels good.

Stay with stroking, kissing, and allow your sensual touching to become more sexual in nature. Pay attention to how your partner likes to be touched, so you can incorporate that knowledge into future love-making when all the options are back on the menu again.

Week Four: Repeating What You Enjoyed Most
Go back and repeat the week that worked best for you. The other element to add is a discussion of what you've learnt about yourself, your partner and your love-making. So you don't just agree with each other, write down your discoveries on a piece of paper and then share them with your partner.

Think ahead to where you go from here. When you reintroduce the sex act into your love-making is there anything that you want to change? I find the following additional questions help my clients to open up:

- What are you embarrassed to ask for during sex?
- What do you wish I would do more of?
- How can I tell you that I'm interested in sex?
- What turns you off?

EXERCISE

Turn your bedroom into a sensual space

Take a fresh look at where you make love and decide you need to make some changes.

De-clutter. Has your bedroom become a dumping ground? Consider whether flu remedies, folders from work and bills on the bedside table are conducive to an intimate atmosphere. Also, a surprising number of clients tell me that they are inhibited by family snapshots on the walls. For this reason photos of your children or parents are best displayed away from the bedroom.

Create the right atmosphere for love-making. Many bedrooms can be a bit feminine (think pink, flowery, and lots of pleated fabric) or childlike (stuffed animals). What sort of sexual energy does this create? Is there anything present that might inhibit one or both of you? Agree together what changes would enhance the bedroom being a shared, loving space.

Is your bedroom warm enough? Nothing is less likely to get you in the mood for good love-making than being cold. If your bedroom's chilly temperature is cooling your ardour perhaps be prepared to have the central heating turned on a little more, or get a heater for instant warmth.

Improve the lighting. Scientists have discovered that making love exclusively in the dark or with harsh, artificial lighting deprives us of a natural sexual stimulant to the brain called oxytocin – produced in the pineal and pituitary gland – which is vital for arousal. So try to create natural and soft lighting in your bedroom.

Use music as soundproofing. Installing a sound system in the bedroom is another good tip for reducing your fear of being overheard and for creating the right mood.

Stimulate all your senses. Don't overlook the importance of smell. This can range from opening a window for fresh air to scented candles, air ionisers, and incense. Think of everything possible to stop your bedroom from being the 'bored' room.

CLOSING THOUGHT

'Once you label me, you negate me.' Danish philosopher Søren Kierkegaard (1813–1855)

It is very easy to label your partner when it comes to sex – for example, 'not interested' or 'stuck in a groove' or 'obsessed'. However, this will stop you from being curious about why he or she has reached this place. It will stop you from seeing evidence that conflicts with your label. Worse still, it stops you from asking about your own attitudes to sex. Sometimes it is easier to criticise your partner rather than face your own contribution to your relationship's sexual problems.

CHAPTER FOUR

Twenty questions to fall in love again

Psychologists have always been interested in how people fall in love. However, more than twenty years ago, American psychologist Dr Arthur Aron decided to take it one stage further and see if he could make two strangers fall in love – just by answering a series of questions together. What was particularly interesting is that two of the participants did fall in love and six months later invited all the researchers to their wedding.

In essence what Dr Aron was trying to do was accelerate intimacy – a bit like students do at university, when they form deep bonds fast by staying up all night with their new friends, talking about their lives, the universe and everything.

I've decided to adapt Dr Aron's questions, and added many of my own, with the aim of bringing back intimacy to long-term couples who have lost sight of each other or started to take each other for granted.

In many ways, going through my twenty questions together will be like going on a first date – all over again. Remember how conversation then flowed like wine – it was because you were curious about each other and wanted to tell and know everything. Fast forward ten, fifteen, thirty years and you think your partner can no longer surprise you. Unfortunately, that sort of familiarity breeds boredom.

To understand the full impact, it helps to look at the parallels between love and music. In 1987, William Gaver and George Mandler, psychologists from the University of California, found that the frequency of listening to a certain kind of music increases the preference for it – up to a point. Too much familiarity is a turn-off, especially if the composition is simple. But the more complex the music, the less likely it is for boredom to set in. It's the same with your partner: the more you know about him or her, the more depth of character you perceive, the more fascinating he or she becomes. That's where my twenty questions come in; they are going to help you rediscover each other – and fall in love all over again.

PREPARATION IS KEY

There are five elements to get right to maximise the power of this exercise:

> *Location.* Dress up and get out of the house – so you're not interrupted by children – and switch off your phones. I would suggest going to a wine bar or pub, so it feels like a first date. In a restaurant, there's the distraction of eating and staff clearing plates, which could break the intimacy.
>
> *An open mind.* You don't need to believe that these questions will deepen or rekindle your love. However, I do need you to be open to the experience and to answer the questions as fully and in as much detail as possible. Be curious about your partner's answers. I've included some supplementary questions or you could just nod your head as this will encourage him or her to say more.
>
> *Pretend your partner hasn't heard this before.* Even if the questions ask for stories that you've told before, imagine your partner is hearing them for the first time (like on a date). When I ask my clients to talk about their childhood during counselling, it is seldom that anything new comes up. However, they find hearing everything in one go and putting all the pieces together provides fresh insight into each other. So don't be afraid to say what seems obvious.

Time. It will take at least an hour to answer these questions – probably much more. My hope is that you'll look at your watches and wonder where the time went. It is perfectly possibly that you will only get through one set of questions on your first date.

Eye contact. Harvard psychologist Zich Rubin found couples in love spend 75% of their time looking into each other's eyes – rather than the usual 30 to 60%. So look at each other, maybe start by holding hands across the table, and if your partner gets emotional, squeeze his or her hand. In this way, you will have good body language too.

THE TWENTY QUESTIONS

Each comes with an explanation of what I'm trying to achieve and how to explore the topic further. Like Dr Aron, I have divided them up into three sections so they get progressively more intimate. Once you've read this section, discuss the idea of doing them with your partner, but try not to think about your answers until you get together as I'd like you to be spontaneous and say what feels right in the moment – looking into your partner's eyes.

Section One: General

Q1: If you were stranded with someone in the jungle who, beyond me, would you like it to be?
Why?: This is a simple warm-up question.
Take it further: How do you think each other would cope in the jungle? How well would your two choices of companion get on together?

Q2: In what period in history would you like to have lived and why?
Why?: Shines a light into your interests and dreams.
Take it further: What do you think your choices reveal about each other?

Q3: If you could have a superpower what would it be?
Why?: It's a graphic way of revealing what we find hard.
Take it further: I've had clients who wanted to be invisible because they always felt in the wrong as a child or who wanted to be made of rubber, so they could bend in the ways other people expected. So why do you think your – and your partner's – chosen superpower is so appealing?

Q4: What would be your perfect day from waking up in the morning to falling asleep at night?
Why?: We think we know what our partner likes but do we really?

Take it further: At this point, I'd like you to simply imagine the day but you could take it further and actually do it. In fact, I have an exercise where I ask couples to take it in turns to be king and queen. This is how it works. During your day, for men as king and woman as queen, you design all the shared activities to your personal taste, and your partner (your loyal subject) goes along with them with good grace. Not only do your choices reveal a lot about your personality but this gets round the problem of couple time always being a compromise between two different tastes and you'll see more clearly what your partner likes or dislikes.

Q5: If you could ask one of your grandparents or your parents one thing, who would you choose and what would it be?

Why?: To examine your relationship with key people in your life through fresh eyes.

Take it further: What families *don't* talk about is always interesting and shines a light into ways you were made to conform as children to rules of which you were only half aware.

Q6: For what in your life – beyond marriage and children – do you feel most grateful?

Why?: We seldom stop and count our blessings; this is a good opportunity.

Take it further: People are often more focused on what they don't have rather than what they do. Consider if you fall into this trap and if so, what the impact is on those around you.

Section Two: Personal

Q7: What do you consider your greatest strength and your greatest weakness?
Why?: A chance to hear your partner's internal chatter.
Take it further: I'm always interested to know which part of the question – whether it's their greatest strength or weakness – my clients find hardest to answer and why.

Q8: What ambitions have you yet to achieve?
Why?: Looks into the future.
Take it further: I believe it's important to review your life every so often or you're living on auto-pilot and when you turn round ten years have gone by – and that leads to resentment or even a midlife crisis. A good follow-up question to ask yourself or your partner is: why haven't you achieved them yet?

Q9: Tell your life story from childhood to today in about five minutes.
Why?: The stories we tell ourselves shape many of our choices and reactions to adversity. This is a chance to get your core narrative out in the open and really hear it yourself (and maybe for the first time admit it to yourself).

Take it further: Look at the recurrent themes. Is it an ascending narrative (everything getting better) or a descending one (getting worse) or does it have ups and downs (which is probably more realistic)? What surprised you about your own story and what did you feel while listening to your partner's?

Q10: What is the most terrible memory from your childhood?
Why?: This is perhaps the most personally revealing question as our childhood shapes the adult we become.
Take it further: Look at how and why this moment still resonates today.

Q11: Do you have a secret hunch about how you will die?
Why?: Introduces the fact that we're not going to live forever and therefore need to make every second count together rather than settling for an OK or even disappointing relationship.
Take it further: A chance to examine your fears and anxieties. Does it help to look ahead or is it better to live in blissful ignorance? If a fortune teller could predict when you'd die, would you like to know?

Q12: What gives your life meaning?
Why?: A question that everybody should ask themselves, especially in middle age when we look back at the first half of our life and forward into the second half, otherwise we

lose sight of ourselves and get bogged down doing things that drain rather than feed us.

Take it further: Knowing what drives your partner allows you to tell the difference between simple wants and fundamental needs and be a team to help each other live more meaningfully. Have you thought about this question before? What feelings does it elicit?

Section Three: Your Relationship

In this section take turns to ask the question first and try not to duplicate your partner's answers.

Q13: What qualities did I possess that made you think I was someone special?

Why?: It's a question I often ask my clients in the first session to remind them of their special bond.

Take it further: How do you feel about those qualities now? Has what first attracted you at the beginning become an issue today? For example, did you like your partner's outgoing personality but today feel he or she is not focused enough on home and family?

Q14: What was, for you, the most memorable moment of our wedding day or our first date?

Why?: It's a landmark day and a happy memory from which to draw strength.

Take it further: Share other anecdotes from your wedding or when you first met.

Q15: What three things do we have in common?
Why?: A warm-up question to start talking about your relationship today.
Take it further: How have the things we share in common changed over the years? Is this a good or a bad thing?

Q16: When have you been made to feel small and ashamed? Please give an example where I didn't cause the shame and one where I did.
Why?: Shame is the most difficult emotion to cope with – rather than challenging one particular behaviour ('You have left the bathroom in a mess'), it's about our whole personality ('You're lazy' or 'a slob'). That's why I describe shame as the opposite of love (which is about accepting us, warts and all).
Take it further: Thank your partner for being so honest. Sympathise with the pain of the event for which you were not responsible and apologise for pain caused by the one you triggered. Keep good eye contact and be certain to hold hands at this point: it will help lessen the pain involved in answering this question.

Q17: What, if anything, is too serious to be joked about in our relationship?

Why?: It makes you both acknowledge the potential no-go areas.

Take it further: What we don't talk about gathers power in the shadows and becomes more frightening. I'm not asking you to discuss these issues now but please ask each other: How could we address these topics in the future? What would make it easier?

Q18: Complete this sentence: I wish I had someone with whom I could share...

Why?: Begins to look into the future.

Take it further: I should stress that the someone does not have to be your partner. It is good to have separate interests. Please also discuss how you feel about your partner having close friends and if and when each of you feels excluded. What new shared activity might you like to do together?

Q19: If there was one small thing about my behaviour that you'd like me to change, what would it be?

Why?: Leaves you both invested in carrying on the conversation.

Take it further: Try and make these complaints similar in severity, so it feels like a fair trade. For example, when they got married, my mother agreed to stop reading at bedtime and my father to stop dunking his biscuits in his tea.

Q20: Which question was hardest to answer and why?

Why?: An opportunity to look back on the exercise together.

Take it further: If you had tried to guess which your partner found hardest, would you have been correct? What surprised you about your partner's answers? What about your own?

WHEN YOU FINISH

Endings are just as important as beginnings:

- Spend time looking into each other's eyes. Dr Aron asked his volunteers to spend four minutes staring at each other without speaking. I'd like you to do the same.
- Honour the experience. It's up to both of you to decide how. It could be by doing something fun (going to a comedy club) or feeding the senses (buying ice cream).
- Sleep on it. Don't assess the impact on yourself and the relationship immediately. Leave it at least a day or two but set up a time to touch base with each other.

Warning

It will probably take more than one evening to work through all these questions – especially if you follow the ideas in the 'take it further' sections. Don't rush through, take your time. There is no ticking clock. If your partner, or you yourself, gets upset, be patient, compassionate and tell yourself it's just a passing emotion, you can sit with it and everything will be OK.

Speak Your Partner's Love Language

If you wanted to communicate with someone Japanese you'd probably hire an interpreter and study the culture. However, when we fall in love we assume our partner has exactly the same way of communicating romantically as we do. During the honeymoon phase, any differences do not matter as our whole focus is on our beloved. The problems come later, when everyday life intrudes and we have less time to devote to the relationship. That's fine if your partner's way of showing love is the same as yours, but the catch is there are five different 'languages' of love. So how do you express your love – and does it match the way your other half expresses theirs?

Creating Quality Time Together

This can range from lying in each other's arms while watching TV through to exotic foreign holidays. You'll become fed up if your partner spends too much time on friends, hobbies or at work. You'll complain: 'We never have any fun together' or 'You've got time for everybody but me', The worst thing your partner could do would be to put off a 'date' or 'family day out' to catch up on chores or cancel because a friend needs him or her.

> **If this is your partner:** The event is less important than spending time together but make certain that you are truly focused on your partner and not just sharing your time, but your thoughts too.

Caring Actions

Sometimes these can be basic partnership tasks like earning
a good salary or keeping a nice house but normally they are
more intimate – cooking a three-course meal, helping your
partner clean out the shed or taking his or her sister to the
airport. You are most likely to say: 'Actions speak louder than
words'. The worst thing your partner could do would be not
finishing that little job he or she promised.

> **If this is your partner:** If you're uncertain what to do,
> listen to what your partner complains about. At the
> moment this will feel like being nagged but look for a twist
> to turn it into a demonstration of your love. For example,
> the complaint might be a messy bathroom. Don't just tidy
> up, but buy small votive candles and run him or her a hot
> bath too.

Affectionate Physical Contact

Sex immediately springs to mind, but often the hugs and
spontaneous kisses are more important. You adore back-rubs
and massages and are most likely to say: 'Come here and give
us a kiss'. Naturally you are devastated if your partner pushes
you off because he or she is too busy doing something else.

> **If this is your partner:** It works best when it is taken
> out of the sexual arena. For example, the hand in the small
> of your partner's back as you guide her through the door,

stroking the back of his hand as you watch a movie together or a kiss on the nape of the neck as you pass in the hall. Feedback is particularly important for this language, so don't be afraid to ask which contacts were appreciated and which felt uncomfortable or ill-timed.

Appreciative Words

If anybody is likely to write romantic poetry it is going to be you. You want the whole world to know your partner is special by dedicating a song to 'the love of my life' at the local karaoke bar. You are most likely to say: 'I love you', and be upset if your partner brushes it off with 'You're just saying that…'

If this is your partner: Compliments are very important as your partner wants you to be a cheerleader, urging him or her on to even higher achievements. It is not just work, but chores about the house and arranging social events all need praise: 'Thank you for choosing such an interesting play' or 'You got a really smooth finish on the paintwork'. Your partner will also enjoy giving compliments too so make certain that you graciously accept them and say thank you.

Present Giving

From an expensive piece of jewellery through to a chocolate bar bought on the way home, you love to surprise your partner and will go to great lengths to pull off a stunt. You are most likely to say: 'I saw this and thought of you', The worst thing your partner can do is not appreciate the gift or dismiss it: 'I don't need one of those'.

> **If this is your partner:** Our culture is obsessed with the value of presents and has forgotten their true message: 'This is something to say that I've been thinking about you'. Cutting an appropriate picture out of a magazine and making your own card can be a hundred times more effective than automatically buying the same old perfume. Don't wait, either, for a special occasion; lots of little presents will make your partner feel especially loved. If you're not a natural present giver get advice, either from people who know your partner's tastes or from the shop assistant. Look at the type of gifts that your partner gives as this will provide clues for what makes acceptable presents.

WHY YOU NEED TO PLAY TOGETHER

When we were children, play was at the centre of our lives. It is how we learned to interact with our siblings and friends, tried out new skills, developed our imagination and learnt to cooperate. However, when we become adults and committed to the serious business of earning a living, play is relegated to a guilty pleasure (i.e. a round of golf on a Sunday afternoon). Of course we play but with our children, with our nieces and nephews or as part of a personal hobby but seldom if ever, with our partner. No wonder your relationship feels stale – you're not having enough fun together. Look down the list of the types of play and think which ones you would enjoy:

Cultural play: Be a tourist in your own area. Go to the theatre, a concert or a lecture.

Entertainment play: Go out and sing karaoke together, go dancing, visit an antiques or craft fair, go bowling or watch a sporting event together (not one where your children are playing).

Great outdoors: Go to the seaside and skim stones over the waves, go for a long ramble, go canoeing, bike trekking, play tennis, go bird watching or spend a weekend in a tent together.

Learn something new together: Take a stand-up comedy class, try snowboarding, climbing, windsurfing or enrol your dog in agility classes.

Put it into action

Make up a list of four things that you would like to do – perhaps from the list or ideas of your own – and ask your partner to choose one. (Try to find a range of activities because it's only fun and play if both of you are enjoying yourselves and finding something from each section should provide something for any taste and interest.) Ask your partner to do the same and choose one of his or her ideas that you'd like to do.

EXERCISE

Watch your words

You think that because your partner loves you that he or she will overlook your black moods or understand that you're just tired and irritable. However, if you stopped and really thought about it, you'd probably know that you've been doing major damage to your relationship. That's why I want you to contemplate this famous inspirational quote.

'Watch your thoughts, they become words;
Watch your words, they become actions;
Watch your actions, they become habits;
Watch your habits, they become character;
Watch your character, for it becomes your destiny'.

So how does it apply to relationships?

'Watch your thoughts, they become words
Watch your words, they become actions
Watch your actions, they become habits
Watch your habits, they undermine your relationship'.

CLOSING THOUGHT

'Some people have many different lives with the same person, others live the same life over with different people.'
British novelist Elizabeth Jane Howard (1923–2014)

So what is Howard saying? First, if you don't learn from history, you're doomed to repeat it but second, (and more interestingly) that you will change over time and your relationship needs to have room to accommodate these alterations. I would add that rather than trying to unilaterally impose those changes on your partner, you need to learn the skills of listening and negotiating.

My seven most powerful interventions

To finish, I'm going to summarise what I consider the seven most important ideas in this book and my most powerful strategies for turning round your relationship.

1 When you've got something difficult to say use this formula: *I feel... when you... because.*

2 Imagine every word your partner says is true because from his or her standpoint it will be.

3 Don't label your partner: be curious about why he or she behaves in this way.

4 Increase the amount of casual touching (without angling for sex).

5   Look at each other when you're speaking to each other
    and have phone-free places (like the bedroom) and
    times (like when you're having a meal together).

6   Look for win-win situations where you both get
    something you want. For example, you could do a trade,
    I will go to *this* if you will do *that*.

7   Have more fun together.

_____

CLOSING THOUGHT

'The person who is best suited to us is not the person who
shares our every taste (he or she doesn't exist), but the
person who can negotiate differences in taste intelligently.'
British writer and philosopher, Alain de Botton

Rather than 'working' on your relationship, which makes
it seem like a slog, develop good habits – like breaking off
what you're doing when your partner comes home and
greeting him or her. Once habits are properly established,
they will happen without you thinking about them and
make a fundamental difference to how you feel about each
other.

Recruit your partner to try again

In an ideal world, your partner would be pleased that you've gone to all the trouble to find, read and share a book on how to improve your relationship. However, I'm well aware that he or she may have a totally different reaction. Perhaps your partner is too hurt or angry to listen, maybe he or she is hearing your overtures as criticism (because your partner was brought up in a family that flung blame about and he or she expects to be labelled as 'the problem') or alternatively, he or she thinks your relationship is beyond repair. So if that's the case, what should you do? Obviously, it would be counter-productive to just hand your partner the book – even if he or she 'agreed' to read it, the chances of this happening are slight or he or she would open it with a closed mind. Fortunately, I have an alternative suggestion.

HOW TO LAY THE GROUND

Whether your partner is relatively receptive or completely uncooperative, the following steps will help you maximise the chances of a positive conversation about this book.

> *Adopt an idea yourself:* Rather than waiting for your partner to be on board, you can start to make changes yourself. Look back over the book and decide on *one* thing that you could do differently to improve your relationship. It needs to be something that you could do over and over again – perhaps one of my seven most powerful strategies.
>
> *Allow enough time for it to bed in:* It will take a while for your changes to bear fruit but if you're strong and don't give up when you don't immediately get a positive response, slowly the atmosphere in the house will improve and your partner will begin to thaw.
>
> *Find the right time to talk:* You need to pick a neutral time – rather than just after a row. I would suggest waiting until you can have what is called a sideways discussion. This is when you're doing something else and not facing each other, which can be confrontational. Good examples of sideways discussions would be when you're gardening together or on a long car journey. Under these circumstances, there are natural breaks in the conversation – so you can think or take a couple of deep breaths – and there is less chance of one or other of you wandering off.

Introduce the book: Ask your partner if he or she has noticed any changes recently. If he or she hasn't registered anything don't be downhearted, explain what you've been trying to do differently. (If you do this calmly and kindly, I'm sure your partner will have noticed but thought you were referring to fundamental changes rather than first steps.) Explain that you have read this book, you've found it helpful – give a couple of examples – and you've adopted one idea already.

Listen to your partner: Rather than trying to counter your partner's doubts or use me to explain why you're right and he or she is wrong, nod your head. This will encourage your partner to say more. Ask an open question about something your partner has said. (Open questions start with how, why, what, when, who...) Use the three most useful words for communication: 'Tell me more'. You might find your partner will begin to answer some of his or her doubts. More importantly, your partner will feel heard, that his or her opinions count and you're not just trying to impose your solution.

Come up with a plan together: Ask open questions like: 'What do we need to do differently?' or 'What changes could we make?' Maybe my book can be part of this process or perhaps you'll come up with something different together. After all, two heads are better than one and you know your relationship better than me. If the conversation becomes heated and negative, suggest that you come back to the topic later.

CLOSING THOUGHT

'Love is in the heart of everyone. It is that spark which animates all life. Feeling love, touching love, weaving it, is that which makes for change.' American maggid (a sacred storyteller) and healer, Andrew Ramer

If you approach your partner with love, kindness and compassion – rather than a list of his or her faults – you are laying the foundation for a better and more loving relationship rather than just putting a lick of paint on the old one.

Further Reading

ANDREW G. MARSHALL

I LOVE YOU
BUT I'M NOT
IN LOVE WITH YOU
Seven Steps to Saving
Your Relationship

I Love You But I'm Not in Love With You

Over 100,000 copies sold worldwide. This book will help you get to the roots of why seemingly loving partners detach and how the simple everyday things you thought were protecting your relationship were really undermining it. There is more information about limerence and how to speak your partner's love language. Also includes:

- How to argue productively and address the core of the issue
- Employ the trigger words for more effective communication
- Find a balance between being fulfilled as an individual and being one half of a couple
- Create new bonds instead of searching for old ones

Have The Sex You Want

If your sex life is more about going through the motions than building connection, this book is for you. It will develop the ideas in chapter three of this book and provides more in-depth information about my plan for restoring intimacy. Also includes:

- Deal with different levels of desire
- Combat the unhelpful myths about men and women and sex
- Repair the damage from an affair by reconnecting again in the bedroom

What is Love?

Love is one of the most powerful forces in our lives but it is also one of the most misunderstood. This book combines some of the great minds who have written about love from across the ages plus fifty letters from people just like you. Many of my clients read this book with their partner because it prompts useful discussions about love and relationships without getting caught in the same old loops. If you found the 20 Questions to Fall in Love Again in this book helpful to get you talking, take it in turns to read out the letters and each answer them – then read what I have said and discuss. Sections include:

- The spark went out
- Doubts about being in love
- Making amends
- Restoring love after an affair

Wake Up and Change Your Life

If your problems are more fundamental, I have nine ideas that build into a proven plan for personal transformation (which in turn could transform your relationship). There's an explanation of why change is so tough and how to discover what's really holding you back. Most important, for when you're in crisis, there's advice on how to keep calm. The book also features:

- Everything you need to know about improving the way that you communicate
- The importance of boundaries for you and your relationships
- Understanding the difference between your zone of concern and your zone of control
- An in-depth explanation about Mindfulness and living in the present

My Wife Doesn't Love Me Any More

If your life is in turmoil because you wife has just told you that she doesn't love you and your marriage is over, this book will bring a bit of sanity into your world. In my experience, more relationships end at this point not because women are determined to leave but because men panic and end up pushing their wives further even further away. In this book, I explain how to keep calm and listen, really listen rather than arguing or trying to find a magic fix. I also cover:

- How to figure out why she's fallen out of love
- Five things you think will save your relationship but you should absolutely avoid
- What her words and actions really mean and how to use them to win her back
- What to do to instantly improve the atmosphere at home
- How to prevent past mistakes from undermining your attempts to build a better future

My Husband Doesn't Love Me And He's Texting Someone Else

Men fall out of love for different reasons to women and this book will explain the three things every woman needs to know to protect her relationship. It is also full of practical techniques for coming back from the brink and advice on diagnosing whether your husband is depressed (plus what to do if he is). In the second half of the book, I tackle what to do if you suspect or know your husband is having an affair:

- The six types of other woman, from 'a spark' to 'the love of his life'
- Tailored strategies for dealing with each type
- Five worst and best reactions after uncovering what's really going on
- How to combat the poison that she's slipping into your relationship
- When to keep fighting and when to make a tactical withdrawal

ANDREW G. MARSHALL

How Can
I Ever
Trust You
Again?

INFIDELITY
From Discovery
to Recovery in
Seven Steps

How Can I Ever Trust You Again?

If your partner has had an affair my best-selling book covers the seven stages of recovery. It will help make sense of your feelings and reassure you that they are normal and understandable. There's also my detailed plan on how to come out of this crisis with a stronger and better marriage. Each chapter ends with a short section written for the partner who has been unfaithful and many couples find these prompt constructive conversations on how to move forward helpful. The book also includes:

- The eight types of affairs and how understanding your partner's is key to rescuing your relationship
- How to stop your imagination running wild and your brain going into meltdown
- How the person who had the affair can help their partner recover
- What derails recovery and how to get your marriage on track again

It's Not a Midlife Crisis, It's An Opportunity

If you think your partner is having a midlife crisis but even suggesting the idea makes him or her angry and resentful, you'll find this book really helpful. If it's your life that no longer makes sense and you're looking to make big changes, it will help you take stock, understand how you got to this place and make a considered plan for the future. Whichever side of the divide you stand on, this book offers:

- A whole new vocabulary for discussing the midlife crisis without alienating each other
- What causes depression and what is a helpful and an unhelpful reaction
- Five killer replies to the blocks that stop you talking properly about your marriage
- Why if you pass the midlife test everything is up from here

Titles by Andrew G. Marshall

ANDREW G. MARSHALL

ARE YOU RIGHT FOR ME?

Seven steps to getting clarity and commitment in your relationship

BLOOMSBURY

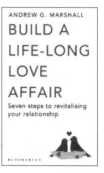

ANDREW G. MARSHALL

BUILD A LIFE-LONG LOVE AFFAIR

Seven steps to revitalising your relationship

BLOOMSBURY

ANDREW G. MARSHALL

HEAL AND MOVE ON

Seven steps to recovering from a break-up

BLOOMSBURY

ANDREW G. MARSHALL

RESOLVE YOUR DIFFERENCES

Seven steps to dealing with conflict in your relationship

BLOOMSBURY

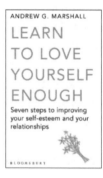

ANDREW G. MARSHALL

LEARN TO LOVE YOURSELF ENOUGH

Seven steps to improving your self-esteem and your relationships

BLOOMSBURY

ANDREW G. MARSHALL

HELP YOUR PARTNER SAY 'YES'

Seven steps to achieving better cooperation and communication

BLOOMSBURY

ANDREW G. MARSHALL
Author of I Love You But I'm Not in Love With You

I LOVE YOU BUT YOU ALWAYS PUT ME LAST

How to childproof your marriage

ANDREW G. MARSHALL

I LOVE YOU BUT I'M NOT IN LOVE WITH YOU

Seven Steps to Saving Your Relationship

BLOOMSBURY

BLOOMSBURY
ANDREW G. MARSHALL

How Can I Ever Trust You Again?

INFIDELITY: From Discovery to Recovery in Seven Steps

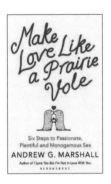

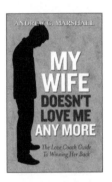

Visit www.andrewmarshall.com

About the Author

Andrew G. Marshall is a marital therapist with thirty years experience. He trained with RELATE (the UK's leading couples' counselling charity) but now leads a team in private practice in London and Sussex offering the Marshall Method. He is also the author of eighteen other books on relationships and contributes to the *Mail on Sunday*, *Sunday Telegraph, The Times* and women's magazines around the world. To date, his work has been translated into over twenty different languages. To receive regular updates about Andrew's books, articles and events subscribe to his newsletter at www.andrewgmarshall.com